THE LEADERSHIP LANGUAGE

*Leadership is not about being in charge.
It's about taking care of those in your charge.*
Simon Sinek

THE LEADERSHIP LANGUAGE

Guide To Fostering Authentic Relationships
Inspiring Trust & Genuine Connections

T.W. Reel III

Table of Contents

CHAPTER 1: What is the Leadership Language? 1

CHAPTER 2: The Psychology of Leadership and Connection 10

CHAPTER 3: Confirmation Affirmation 15

CHAPTER 4: Being of Service 26

CHAPTER 5: Recognition 32

CHAPTER 6: Time Spent, Time Valued 43

CHAPTER 7: Personalized Presence 51

CHAPTER 8: Consideration 59

CHAPTER 9: Integrating the Leadership Language 68

CHAPTER 10: Sustaining and Adapting Long-Term Strategies 77

CHAPTER 11: Wrap-Up & Final Thoughts 84

CHAPTER 1

What is the Leadership Language?

"In this ever-changing society, the most powerful and enduring brands are built from the heart. They are real and sustainable. Their foundations are stronger because they are built with the strength of the human spirit, not an ad campaign."

- HOWARD SCHULTZ
Former CEO of Starbucks

There's a four-letter word that doesn't get much attention in the professional world, mainly because of its personal connotation. This word can take on multiple meanings and is often interpreted as the result of personal relationships, leading to the use of non-corporate, unfriendly terms such as romance or intimacy. Before you contact your HR department to set off alarm bells, please keep in mind that this four-letter word means no harm. In fact, it is a very powerful word that, if demonstrated correctly (and ethically), will have a profound impact on your ability to lead, build relationships, and establish trust. You've probably already guessed it. Are you ready? Hold your horses, and make sure all arms and legs are inside the vehicle at all times.

The word is **LOVE**.

Whew! Are you still with me? You haven't closed the book yet? Ok good. Now that we are past that initial shock, let me explain. This word has many definitions and interpretations, but for this book and your leadership development, consider this one. Love refers to the culture of care, respect, and genuine concern for the well-being of employees. When integrated into leadership and organizational practices, love can significantly enhance employee engagement, satisfaction, and overall performance.

Why does this matter?

To truly establish a valuable leadership legacy, love must be present in the way we act and communicate throughout our relationships with individuals and work. As leaders, our role is to bring the best out of our teams by empowering them to succeed and creating an environment where they can thrive. We, as leaders, set the tone for what that looks like. Leaders often acquire this knowledge through their personal experiences under the guidance of others. You put into practice things you liked, and you also remember to avoid some things you didn't like. While this is significant and valuable, it is only one aspect of the overall picture. Ultimately, we perceive our leadership abilities and experience solely based on our own understanding.

To be clear, I don't want to discredit that. Each leader has their own unique flavor that can resonate well with teams and individuals. However, this development and relationship building can take a tremendous amount of time, which, for leaders, can be a luxury. In a perfect world, it would be awesome if all we did was help grow individuals to become the best versions of themselves. As you and I both know, that's almost impossible to achieve. However, leaders still have deadlines, tasks, and responsibilities that consume their time. The more we pour into our own work, the less time we get to lead others. Instead, we become task managers, making sure to check off those to-do lists and stay ahead of those deadlines.

We have to find a balance. If we fail to strike a balance, the perception we create for our team could result in a lack of growth and stagnation. This could be due to our failure to take the time to learn about our employees, understand their concerns, and find ways to integrate them into the larger picture. Nobody wants to feel compartmentalized by their leader. Meaning no one wants to be put into a box, in this case a check box, feeling like a requirement or obligation to be led by their supervisor. Employees may perceive this as a requirement or obligation, leading them to yearn for words like authenticity, genuineness, and appreciation.

So, where do we begin? How can we stop this vicious cycle of trying to be the ultimate task master?

It all starts with our language and how it conveys meaning to our relationships. Our language can demonstrate how we want our culture to be known as a leader. It is much more than just communication. It is a form of expression that is open to embracing the diverse dialects of each person's unique characteristics and experiences. It is a living entity, changing over time to meet the cultural shifts and priorities of new relationship dynamics.

You are the maestro for this symphony of expression, waving your baton and setting the tone for how your musicians (employees) will respond to your guidance and leadership, while at the same time respecting their abilities, experience, and preferences. This could be your first time as a conductor (leader), or you are a veteran leader looking to refresh your skills. Whatever the case, I encourage you to keep this book as you grow in your leadership. We need to check in with ourselves, making sure that we continuously improve and remain aligned with our reason and purpose for being leaders.

After reading this book, my goal and hope is that you not only find value in its content, but also share it forward to others. Again, a word I used at the beginning was for you to become invaluable. You are the sharer of knowledge and skills, leaving a legacy of the leadership language evident in your culture as you help others grow in their leadership, demonstrating that misunderstood but powerful four-letter word: love.

What is the Leadership Language?

So, what is the Leadership Language? They are principles that promote and encourage actionable consideration of the differences in what employees need or want in order to have an enriching work relationship with their leader. This impacts how leaders build relationships with each employee that fit the dynamic and norms of each individual, creating a more fulfilling work environment that leads to greater individual empowerment, team culture, and value-driven success. Whew, that's a mouthful! In essence, as a leader, you strive to understand the unique needs of each employee and establish a relationship that fosters their best potential.

Once you know what their leadership language preferences are, you can act in that way to fulfill the employee's needs or wants, making their work experience and success that much better. You can leverage these relationship priorities to help guide and empower them to achieve team goals or strategic efforts. Change is constant, but change is also hard. Knowing how to use your Leadership Language can provide the fulfillment needed to keep those employees going, knowing they have a leader who "gets me" and has my back, even when times are tough.

How do I know if it's working?

What are some ways to know if my leadership language efforts are effective?

While there is no one-size-fits-all solution, there are some important factors that can contribute to this. Below is a quick list and descriptions. As you read this list, I want you to examine the current state of your relationship dynamics and team perceptions. Are there any areas that are performing well? Or, is there room for improvement? Here are some signs that you are moving in the right direction.

Fostering Trust and Loyalty
Trust Building: Demonstrated through empathy, transparency, and consistent support builds trust between leaders and employees.
Loyalty: Employees who feel valued and cared for are more likely to stay committed, reducing turnover rates.

Enhancing Employee Engagement
Emotional Connection: Creates an emotional bond between employees and the organization, leading to higher levels of engagement and enthusiasm.
Motivation: When employees feel appreciated, they are more motivated to contribute to the organization's success.

Creating a Positive Work Environment
Workplace Culture: Promotes kindness, cooperation, and mutual respect, resulting in a more harmonious environment.
Conflict Resolution: Encourages open communication and understanding, which can help resolve conflicts amicably.

Improving Mental and Emotional Well-being
Supportive Atmosphere: Manifests as support during challenging times, contributing to employees' mental and emotional well-being.

What is the Leadership Language?

Stress Reduction: A caring environment can alleviate stress and anxiety, leading to better overall health and productivity.

Boosting Creativity and Innovation
Psychological Safety: When employees feel cared for, they are more likely to take risks and share innovative ideas without fear of judgment.
Collaboration: Employees are more willing to work together and support each other's ideas.

Enhancing Leadership Effectiveness
Empathetic Leadership: Leaders can demonstrate empathy and understanding, which can inspire and empower their teams.
Role Modeling: Leaders set a positive example, encouraging similar behaviors throughout the organization.

Strengthening Team Cohesion
Team Spirit: Binds teams together, fostering a sense of unity and collective purpose.
Support Networks: Employees are more likely to support and help each other, enhancing team performance.

Before I introduce the leadership language principles, I want to make one thing clear. This is not just a feel-good concept but a powerful force that can drive organizational success. By fostering trust, engagement, and a positive work environment, The Leadership Language enhances the overall well-being and performance of employees. Leaders who embrace and model this can lay the foundation for a thriving and resilient organization.

What is the Leadership Language?

Also, it is important to remain consistent as you use your Leadership Language. We must humble ourselves to know that there is always something new to learn, and that we are also willing to listen to and learn from others within our team. Trust is key. Gaining trust can be challenging, but regaining it can be even harder. If you're using leadership language correctly, you'll know how to restore employee confidence in you when challenges arise. Are you ready? Here we go! Below are the Leadership Language Principles.

Confirmation Affirmation
Preferred way of recognizing and validating an employee's contributions, opportunities, and potential, strengthening their confidence and commitment

Being of Service
The degree of support and assistance an employee desires, demonstrated in the leader's ability to actively help achieve goals and objectives.

Recognition
Desired level of acknowledgment of employees' achievements and efforts, which fosters motivation, satisfaction, and a sense of value within the team.

Time Spent, Time Valued
Dedicating the appropriate amount of quality time with each employee to address their needs, while validating the time spent provided value towards their priorities.

Personalized Presence

Level of attentiveness and engagement with each employee, understanding their unique needs and preferences, and fostering a deeper, more meaningful connection."

Consideration

Attentively listening to employees' concerns, valuing their perspectives, and making thoughtful decisions that prioritize their well-being and development.

Chapter 2

The Psychology of Leadership and Connection

> *"True leadership stems from individuality that is honestly and sometimes imperfectly expressed... Leaders should strive for authenticity over perfection".*
>
> **- SHERYL SANDBERG**
> Former COO of Facebook

Let's dive into the psychology behind effective leadership and employee engagement, shall we? Hold onto your hats because we're about to unpack what might seem like a heap of complex theories but are really the stepping stones to mastering your "leadership language."

The Real Deal with Psychological Needs

Picture this: At the core of stellar employee engagement and leadership lies the simple concept of meeting basic psychological needs. You might be wondering what these are. Well, according to the fancy term "Self-Determination Theory," or SDT for short, it's all about autonomy, competence, and relatedness.

Autonomy - This isn't about going rogue; it's about giving your team the reins to steer their own ship at times. Imagine empowering your crew with choices and the freedom to initiate things. Sounds good, right?

Competence - Here, it's all about feeling like you've got the chops to get the job done. As a leader, you boost this by throwing challenges that are just tough enough and giving out praise that's not just fluff but genuine recognition.

Relatedness - Ever felt like you just belong? That's relatedness in a nutshell. Creating an environment where everyone feels part of what's going on instead of just going along for the ride. Think supportive, open, and, yeah, kind of warm and fuzzy.

Emotional Intelligence: Not Just Buzzwords

Now, let's talk about Emotional Intelligence (EI). If leadership were a video game, EI would be the cheat code. It's about knowing your emotions, managing them, reading the room, and handling relationships with a precise touch. Here's the breakdown:

Self-awareness: Knowing your own emotional ups and downs.

Self-regulation: Keeping those emotions in check.

Social awareness: Picking up on others' feelings.

Relationship management: Navigating interactions like a pro.

The Secret Sauce: Psychological Safety

Remember Google's Project Aristotle? No, it's not a history lesson, but a real gem about what makes teams tick. Top of the list? Psychological safety. It's about creating a safe space for taking risks without feeling like you're walking a tightrope without a net. In the realm of modern leadership, the concept of psychological safety has emerged as a cornerstone for building effective teams and fostering a positive workplace culture. Psychological safety, coined by Amy Edmondson of Harvard Business School, describes a team climate characterized by interpersonal trust and mutual respect in which people feel comfortable being themselves and expressing themselves without fear of negative consequences. Integrating this principle into the leadership language improves not only team dynamics but also an organization's overall effectiveness.

Strategies to Enhance Psychological Safety

To enhance psychological safety across these leadership dimensions, leaders can employ several strategies:

> **Encourage Open Dialogue**: Foster an environment where team members feel safe to express their thoughts and ideas without fear of judgment. Promote discussions that welcome diverse viewpoints and invites everyone to speak.
>
> **Normalize the Learning from Failures:** Foster a culture that views mistakes as learning opportunities rather than punishments. This approach helps to alleviate the fear of failure, which is crucial for maintaining psychological safety.

Lead by Example: Demonstrate vulnerability by sharing your own challenges and learning experiences. When leaders are open about their own failures and uncertainties, it sets a powerful example for the team, showing that it is safe to admit mistakes and not know all the answers.

Provide Clear Expectations: Uncertainty can undermine psychological safety. Make sure that team members understand their roles, responsibilities, and team goals. Clear communication reduces anxiety and builds confidence.

Tailor-Made Leadership

Every team member is unique, and your leadership should be like a bespoke suit – tailored to fit perfectly. It's about mixing and matching your leadership style to suit everyone's taste. Sometimes you lead from the front, sometimes from the side, and sometimes you just set the stage and let the team shine.

Motivation Station

Here's the skinny on motivation: it's the fuel for the engine. There are two flavors here – intrinsic (from within because it feels good) and extrinsic (for the rewards). The trick is to balance these like a pro DJ mixing tracks. Get it right, and you've got a hit.

Transformational Leadership: Turning It Up to Eleven

This is where you morph from a manager to a leader. Transformational leadership is like being a coach, cheerleader, and chess master all rolled into one. It's about inspiring, pushing boundaries, and treating each team member like the MVP they are.

Wrapping It Up: It's All About L-O-V-E
And here we circle back to that four-letter word – LOVE. Not the mushy stuff, but the real, tough, genuine care and respect that glues a team together. Leading with love isn't just nice; it's necessary.

So, there you have it! The psychology behind effective leadership and employee engagement isn't just about being a boss. It's about being a leader, a listener, and sometimes a friend. Play around with these ideas and see how your "leadership language" can turn your team from clocking in to thriving. Now, don't just sit there; get out and lead like you mean it! Ready to get started? I've kept you waiting long enough. Let's delve into the first principle: Confirmation Affirmation.

Chapter 3

Confirmation Affirmation

"Be hearty in your approbation and lavish in your praise, and people will cherish your words and treasure them and repeat them over a lifetime."

- DALE CARNEGIE
Training & Public Speaking Pioneer

Side Note: In case you were wondering (because I was); the work approbation means commendation or praise. *The more you know!* Alright, let's dive into something truly game-changing in the world of leadership: Confirmation Affirmation.

Now, do not let the fancy term throw you off—this is all about the art of recognizing and validating your team's efforts and potentials in a way that resonates with what each individual wants. It really comes down to two simple words that let your employee know they're working towards the right results in the right way: expectations and direction. Employees want to know what good looks like and why it matters. By providing clarity for the work they do and how it helps the bigger picture, we can provide meaning for how they fit into the organizational equation.

The Power of Clarity in Leadership

Imagine sailing a ship in foggy weather without a compass. Sounds tricky, right? That's exactly how your team feels when expectations aren't clear. As a leader, your job is to clear the fog—giving your team a map by setting clear expectations and a compass to provide the right direction. When employees understand what 'good' looks like and why their work matters, they're not just doing a job; they're fulfilling a mission.

Why Expectations and Direction Matter

Let's break down why these two elements are critical to the recipe for effective leadership:

Boosts Confidence: Team members feel more confident in their roles when expectations are clear. Confidence breeds competence, and competence breeds success.

Enhances Productivity: A clear direction eliminates guesswork. Your team spends less time wondering what they should be doing and more time actually doing it.

Fosters Accountability: When expectations are defined, accountability follows. It becomes easier for team members to hold themselves and each other accountable, driving a culture of high performance.

Confirmation Affirmation

Drives Engagement: Understanding how their work fits into the larger picture gives employees a sense of purpose. Engaged employees aren't just present; they're motivated and passionate.

Setting the Stage: Crafting Clear Expectations

Creating clear expectations isn't just about setting targets. It's about aligning these targets with your organization's broader goals and ensuring that they resonate with your team. Here's how you can ace it:

Be Specific and Measurable: Vague goals breed vague results. Define what success looks like in precise, measurable terms. Instead of saying "improve customer satisfaction," say "increase customer satisfaction ratings by 10% within the next quarter."

Communicate Regularly: Expectations should not be a one-time announcement. Regular communication of expectations is necessary through meetings, one-on-ones, and even informal catch-ups.

Align with Organizational Goals: Connect the dots between individual roles and the organization's objectives. Help your team see how their contributions matter in the grand scheme of things.

Adapt and Update: As business strategies evolve, so should your expectations. Be flexible and ready to update your team on new directions or shifted goals.

Confirmation Affirmation

Steering the Ship: Providing the Right Direction

After setting expectations, your next step is to provide the necessary direction to meet them. This involves more than just delegation; it involves inspiration, guidance, and ongoing support.

Lead by Example: Show, don't just tell. Demonstrate the behaviors and work ethic you expect from your team. If you expect meticulousness and creativity, make sure you're embodying these qualities.

Provide Resources and Tools: Equip your team with the necessary tools, training, and information they need to meet their goals. A well-equipped team is a productive one.

Offer Continuous Feedback: Direction is about course correction. Provide constructive feedback on a regular basis to help your team adjust and improve their trajectory toward meeting expectations.

Encourage Autonomy: While providing direction, also encourage your team to take initiative. Empower them to make decisions within the framework of the expectations you've set.

Overcoming Challenges: Navigating Roadblocks

Setting expectations and providing direction are not without challenges. Here are some common obstacles and how to tackle them:

Confirmation Affirmation

Resistance to Change: Change can be daunting. When introducing new expectations or directions, be clear about the reasons behind them and involve your team in the process.

Miscommunication: Ensure your communication channels are clear and open. Misunderstandings can derail even the best-laid plans.

Overwhelm: Too many changes at once can overwhelm your team. Introduce new expectations gradually and ensure they're manageable.

The Art of Verification: Staying the Course

Let's cut to the chase: verification isn't about micromanaging or breathing down someone's neck. It's about making sure everyone's compass is pointing to True North. As a leader, your role is to confirm that your team's efforts align with the bigger picture. But how do you do it without turning into Big Brother?

Set Clear Expectations: This is your starting line. Clear, concise, and concrete goals are the GPS for your team. Make sure these are well communicated and understood. It's like telling your friend exactly where the party is so they don't end up at the wrong house.

Regular Check-Ins: We don't want death by meeting. That could feel more obligatory, leading to a lack of enthusiasm and participation. Instead, talk to your employee to find out how they prefer to check-in. If it's realistic, go for it. If not, find a way to meet in the middle, and explain why. Make sure meetings are not just to monitor progress but to offer support and guidance. Think of it as a pit-stop in a race where you can refuel and maybe tweak some strategies.

Constructive Feedback Loop: Create an environment where feedback flows both ways. This keeps everyone informed and makes your team feel like they have a voice. Plus, it shows that you're all in this together.

Empowering Individuals: Unleash the Superpowers

Every member of your team has something unique to bring to the table. Your job? Help them see it and use it. Empowering your team means more than just giving them tasks; it's about giving them the reins to make decisions, solve problems, and lead initiatives.

Delegate Meaningfully: Assign tasks that challenge your team members and help them grow. It's like choosing a video game level that's just right—not too easy, not too hard.

Resources and Tools: Equip your team with the right tools for the job. Whether it's training, software, or just some extra time to brainstorm, make sure they have what they need to succeed.

Encourage Autonomy: Trust your team to make decisions. This doesn't mean leaving them to sink or swim; it's about being a safety net while they walk the tightrope.

Confirmation Affirmation

When Things Aren't Peachy: Realigning Efforts

Not every plan is foolproof, and sometimes things go sideways. It's normal. But the real test of leadership is handling these situations with grace and efficiency. Here's how to realign efforts without causing a panic:

> **Early Detection**: Keep an eye on the pulse of your employees. The earlier you catch a misalignment, the easier it is to correct it. It's like noticing you took the wrong exit and quickly taking the next turn to get back on route.

> **Calm and Constructive Approach**: No one likes to hear they're off track, so approach the topic gently. Focus on solutions, not blame. It's like helping someone fix a flat tire rather than scolding them for running over a nail.

> **Collaborative Planning**: Sit down with the team member and map out a plan together. This not only ensures you're both on the same page but also strengthens their commitment to the new direction.

> **Follow-Up Support**: Change can be daunting. Regular check-ins after realigning ensure continued support, and shows your team that you're with them every step of the way.

Let's Get Practical: Making It a Habit

Words of affirmation aren't just about saying "good job" and calling it a day. It's about making your words count, making them specific, and making them resonate. So, how do we do this? Let's break it down.

Communication Techniques That Pack a Punch

Be Specific: When you praise someone, ditch the generics. Be as specific as possible. Instead of saying, "Great job," say, "Great job on that presentation—your approach to explaining our budget breakdown was clear and engaging."

Be Timely: Giving affirmation promptly has the greatest impact. When you see something praiseworthy, say something as soon as possible. This immediate reinforcement helps solidify the behaviors you want to encourage.

Be Public (When Appropriate): Public recognition can amplify the effects of your words, boosting not just the recipient's morale but also setting a positive example for the rest of the team. A shout-out during a team meeting or a mention in a company newsletter can do wonders.

Be Private Too: Some prefer the spotlight not shine too brightly on them. A private note or a quiet compliment can be more appreciated than public praise.

Be Honest: Authenticity is key. Never give hollow or insincere praise. People can sniff out insincerity from a mile away, and it can do more harm than good.

Examples to Get You Going

Example 1: Imagine your team just finished a major project under budget and ahead of schedule. During your next team meeting, take a moment to highlight specific contributions. "I want to thank Julia for her innovative cost-saving strategies and Mark for his extra hours last week to ensure everything was completed ahead of time. Your dedication and clever thinking have set new standards for our team."

Example 2: Let's say a team member handled a difficult client exceptionally well, turning a potential loss into a successful gain. A personal note could read, "Hey Sam, I was really impressed with how you handled Mr. Thompson's concerns on the phone yesterday. Your patience and professionalism didn't just keep his business; I believe it deepened his trust in our company. Fantastic work!"

Exercises for Leaders to Practice

Daily Affirmation Challenge: Challenge yourself to give at least one meaningful affirmation to a team member each day. Make a note of who and what you praise. Review this weekly to ensure you're recognizing a diverse range of contributions.

Affirmation by Walking Around: Make it a habit to stroll around your workplace regularly, looking for opportunities to give positive feedback. This not only helps you spot praiseworthy actions as they happen but also keeps you visibly engaged with your team.

Peer Praise Exercise: During team meetings, encourage team members to give shout-outs to each other. This can foster a positive team culture where affirmation becomes a shared responsibility, not just a leadership duty.

Reflection Sessions: Regularly reflect on the impact your affirmations have. Ask your team members for feedback on how your words impact them. This can help you adjust your approach and become more effective in your affirmations.

Role-Playing Scenarios: During leadership training sessions, practice your affirmation skills through role-playing exercises. This can be especially helpful for those who find giving praise awkward or unnatural.

Tying It All Together:
Confirmation Affirmation as a Leadership Symphony

Each musician (team member) has a part to play, and your job as a leader is to bring out the best in each of them, ensuring they're in harmony with the overall performance. Confirmation Affirmation is your baton—it's what you use to guide, inspire, and sometimes gently correct the course.

Here's a quick recap:

Expectations & Direction are essential: It's the sheet music and tempo that ensure everyone knows how to proceed from start to finish in the right way for the right purpose.

Verification keeps everyone on track: It's about making sure that every note hits the right pitch and that the music flows in the right direction.

Empowerment lets each musician shine: It's about trusting your violinist to take that solo and encouraging the drummers to keep the rhythm pumping.

Realigning is fine-tuning: Every now and then, you might need to tweak the strings or adjust the tempo. It's all part of creating a masterpiece.

Praise always goes to the musicians: Even though leaders conduct, it is the musicians that bring sound to life. Let them take a bow and see your genuine appreciation.

Wrapping It Up with a Bow

So, there you have it. Confirmation Affirmation is about so much more than just making people feel good or looking for mistakes. It's a strategic tool that can boost morale, motivation, and loyalty. It's about creating an environment where people feel valued and seen, which in turn inspires them to keep bringing their best selves to work. And remember: the more authentic and targeted your praise and verification, the more impactful it will be. Now go out there, be bold with your confirmation affirmations, and watch your team soar!

Chapter 4

Being of Service

"Everybody can be great ... because anybody can serve. You don't have to have a college degree to serve. You don't have to make your subject and verb agree to serve. You only need a heart full of grace. A soul generated by love"

- MARTIN LUTHER KING JR.

In this chapter, we're zooming in on a critical aspect of leadership: Being of Service. Now, before you think we're talking about volunteering for the next office potluck, let's set the record straight. Being of Service isn't about doing the work for your team; it's about doing work that supports your team. It's about stepping up, getting your hands dirty, and showing that you're in the trenches with them. Let's dive into why this matters, pepper it with some stellar examples from both the past and present, and tackle those pesky challenges that come along for the ride.

Why Acts of Service?

First things first, why should a leader even bother? Well, it's simple: actions speak louder than words. When leaders jump into action to assist, support, or even alleviate some of the burdens your team faces, you're speaking volumes about your commitment to the group's success and well-being. This isn't just about boosting morale; it's about building trust, enhancing respect, and fostering a culture where everyone feels valued and supported.

The Impact: Building Trust and Respect

Leaders directly influence trust and respect, which are the cornerstones of any successful relationship. When team members see their leader putting in effort to support them—not just delegating but actively contributing—it builds trust in a very organic way. They know their leader isn't just barking orders from a high tower but is right there with them, facing the same challenges.

Historical Examples of Acts of Service in Leadership

History is ripe with leaders whose acts of service have left marks on the sands of time. Let's stroll down memory lane:

> **George Washington**: As the commander of the Continental Army, he was known for riding alongside his men, sharing their hardships, even in the brutal winter at Valley Forge. His willingness to endure the same conditions as his men not only boosted their spirits, but also solidified their loyalty and trust in his leadership.

Mother Teresa: While not a corporate leader, her life was a testament to leadership through service. Her relentless dedication to the care of the sick, poor, and dying in Kolkata provided a powerful model of selfless service and compassionate leadership.

Nelson Mandela: His leadership extended well beyond his presidency. His actions in fostering reconciliation in post-apartheid South Africa demonstrated a profound commitment to serving his nation, emphasizing unity and healing over personal gain.

Contemporary Acts of Service

Moving from the annals of history to the dynamic corridors of today's corporate world, let's see how modern leaders embody this principle:

Satya Nadella at Microsoft: Under his leadership, Microsoft has seen a shift towards a more empathetic workplace culture. Nadella's focus on understanding and addressing the needs of his employees—whether through enhanced parental leave policies or resources for mental health—exemplifies leadership as an act of service.

Indra Nooyi, former CEO of PepsiCo: Known for her hands-on leadership style, Nooyi would often write letters to the parents of her executives, thanking them for the 'gift' of their children. This deeply personal act of gratitude not only endeared her to her team, but also fostered a familial atmosphere at PepsiCo.

Challenges of Acts of Service

While the benefits are plentiful, the path of service isn't without its thorns. Here are a few challenges leaders might face:

Misinterpretation: At times, people may perceive acts of service as insincere or as a PR stunt. Ensuring authenticity in these actions is crucial for them to be effective.

Balancing Service with Authority: Some leaders fear that being too service-oriented might undermine their authority. The key is to balance empathy with decisiveness. You can be supportive while still making tough decisions.

Avoiding Burnout: Leaders who focus heavily on serving others may risk their own well-being. It's vital to set boundaries and take time for self-care to remain effective and avoid burnout.

Ensuring Authenticity: Actions perceived as insincere can backfire. Always ensure that your acts of service come from a genuine place. Authenticity builds trust; without it, even the best initiatives can fail.

Making It Work: The Toolbox of Supportive Actions

Being of service isn't just a lofty ideal; it's a daily commitment that manifests through specific actions and behaviors. Let's break down the essential tools, daily habits, and strategies that can help you foster a culture of support and ensure your team not only survives but thrives.

Active Listening: Make it a point to really listen to your employees. This isn't about waiting for your turn to speak. It's about understanding their concerns, reading between the lines, and acknowledging their feelings and ideas.

Consistent Check-ins: Regular one-on-one meetings can make a world of difference. Use these sessions not just for progress updates but also to ask about challenges they might be facing and support they might need.

Transparency in Communication: Be open about what's happening at higher levels of management. Share what you can, when you can. Uncertainty can be a major stressor, and transparency is key to alleviating anxieties.

Show Support with Results: It's more than just saying, "I'm here for you." It means following through and delivering what you say you will help with. Imagine being the bumpers on a bowling alley lane. Your support helps not only ensure your employees stay out of the gutters, but also realign their efforts to make the strike!

Expect Nothing in Return: A true service-oriented leader is selfless in their actions, understanding that their success is the success of their team. Employees most in need of this attribute may require reassurance that there is no "quid pro quo" or "you scratch my back, I'll scratch yours."

Fostering a Culture of Support

Creating a supportive culture is perhaps the most impactful act of service a leader can undertake. This culture fills every level of the organization and becomes a part of its identity.

Lead by Example: Culture starts at the top. Demonstrate acts of service in your own behavior, and you'll see it echoed by your team and beyond.

Encourage Peer Support: Create an environment where employees feel encouraged to support each other. Recognition can facilitate this by highlighting individual achievements and acts of support among peers.

Provide Resources for Success: Verify your team has access to the resources needed to succeed. This includes emotional and educational resources in addition to physical tools.

Open Door Policy: Maintain an open-door policy that encourages employees to speak freely about their concerns, suggestions, or problems without fear of repercussions.

Conclusion

By embedding supportive actions in your daily habits, engaging in service-oriented activities, and fostering a culture of support, you can transform the way your team operates. This isn't about grand gestures; it's about consistent, genuine acts of service that make your employees feel valued, supported, and empowered.

As a leader, your greatest achievement will be creating an environment where employees not only succeed but also feel genuinely cared for. This is leadership at its finest—leadership that serves, supports, and empowers.

Chapter 5

Recognition
Fostering a Culture of Appreciation

"You never know when a moment and a few sincere words can have an impact on a life."

- ZIG ZIGLAR
American Author and Motivational Speaker

Alright, let's roll up our sleeves and dive into one of the most energizing principles of leadership: Recognition. This isn't just about handing out gold stars or patting folks on the back. We're talking about a fundamental component that sparks motivation, drives satisfaction, and cements a sense of value among your team members. So, buckle up! We're about to explore how strategic recognition can transform your workplace into a buzzing hive of motivated, satisfied, and deeply valued individuals.

The Power of Recognition: More Than Just "Good Job"

Imagine working tirelessly on a project, pouring your heart and soul into it, and once it's done... crickets. Feels pretty lousy, right? Now flip the scene—imagine after all that hard work, your efforts are recognized, your contribution is celebrated, and your value is affirmed. Feels like a shot of adrenaline, doesn't it? That's the power of recognition—it's a fundamental human need and fulfilling this need can amplify a person's drive and engagement at work.

Why Recognition Matters

Before we delve into strategies and stories, let's ground ourselves in the why.

Motivation Booster: Recognition directly impacts motivation. When employees feel recognized, their satisfaction with their job increases, which in turn boosts their willingness to go above and beyond.

Enhances Team Morale: Recognition is contagious. When one team member is recognized, it sets a positive tone across the team, lifting everyone's spirits and encouraging further excellence.

Reduces Employee Turnover: Feeling undervalued is a common reason employees walk away. Regular and meaningful recognition can counteract this by reinforcing their sense of belonging and appreciation.

Strengthens Loyalty: Employees who feel appreciated are more likely to be loyal to their organization. This loyalty translates into longer tenure and deeper company alignment.

Historical and Modern Perspectives on Recognition

Let's draw some inspiration from history and modern practices to see recognition in action:

Historical Glimpse: During the Industrial Revolution, the concept of employee recognition was virtually non-existent. Workers were often seen as just another cog in the machine. Fast forward to the transformative leadership styles of industrialists like Andrew Carnegie, who began to recognize the value of employee welfare and acknowledgment. This shift altered the perception and treatment of workers.

Modern Marvels: Today, companies like Google and Zappos have taken recognition to new heights. Google, for example, uses peer recognition programs that not only empower employees to acknowledge each other's efforts but also tie these recognitions to tangible rewards. Zappos has a whole program dedicated to celebrating employee successes, both big and small, fostering an incredible sense of community and shared success.

Real Talk: Examples from the Trenches

Imagine you've got a team member; let's call her Jamie. Jamie's been burning the midnight oil to get a project finished, and the final product is stellar. Here's where recognition comes into play. Instead of a pat on the back and a quick "thanks," you take a moment in the next team meeting to highlight what Jamie did and why it mattered.

"Team, Jamie's work on Project X not only met our deadline but raised the bar on quality. Her innovative approach and dedication were key to our success. Jamie, your hard work is appreciated and sets a fantastic example for us all."

Ok, but how do I know if that's how they want praise? You have to keep in mind that not everyone wants the red carpet rolled out for them. In fact, some retreat from individual praise. For example, in Japan, it is the cultural norm to not seek individual praise. Japanese society places a strong emphasis on teamwork, rewarding the team rather than the individual. They place such a strong emphasis on teamwork that receiving individual praise would appear awkward and embarrassing. They would alleviate the embarrassment by reinforcing that it was a team effort and not just their individual work that mattered.

Your employees could be like that too. It doesn't have to be a guessing game though. Sometimes, the best thing to do is just ask. Take time during a one-on-one meeting to find out. This also shows consideration (we'll get to that principle later) for what the employee wants. For leaders insistent on rolling out the red carpet, it's ok to recognize their stellar work, but let's ask first. "Hey, you've been killing it, and I want to recognize your efforts in our next all-hands meeting. Would it be okay if I gave a quick shout-out?"

Watch Out: The Pitfalls of Praise

Now, before you start handing out compliments like candy at a parade, let's talk pitfalls. Yes, even something as awesome as praise has its traps. The first is what I like to call "Praise Fatigue." If everyone gets a trophy, then trophies start to lose their shine. Make sure your affirmation is authentic and merited, or it might start to feel hollow.

Another sneaky pitfall is "Mismatched Recognition." This happens when the praise doesn't quite fit the achievement or misses the mark on what the employee values. It's like praising an artist for how quickly they finished a painting when what they really cared about was the emotional depth poured into it. Make sure praise matches not just the achievement but also the values of the person you're praising.

Best Practices in Recognition

Armed with the why and inspired by the who, let's navigate the how. Here are some best practices you can implement to make recognition a powerhouse in your leadership:

> **Timeliness is Key**: Recognize good work as soon as it happens. The closer the recognition is to the action, the more impactful it is.
>
> **Make It Personal and Meaningful**: Tailor the recognition to the individual. What makes one employee beam with pride might not work for another. Personalization demonstrates that you pay attention and care.

Public vs. Private: Know when to give a shout-out in a public forum and when to keep it a low-key, private conversation. Some might relish being in the spotlight, while others might prefer a sincere thank-you in private.

Incorporate Peer Recognition: Facilitate platforms where peers can recognize each other. Peer recognition can often feel as gratifying as recognition from higher-ups, if not more.

Regular and Consistent: Recognition should not be a once-in-a-blue-moon event. Integrate it into your daily and weekly routines to keep the momentum of motivation and satisfaction up.

Overcoming Challenges in Recognition

Now, recognition might sound like a no-brainer, but it comes with its own set of challenges. Let's address some of these with practical solutions:

Avoiding Recognition Fatigue: Yes, too much of a good thing can become ineffective. Keep your recognition efforts genuine and varied to avoid diluting their impact.

Budget Constraints: Not all recognition needs to break the bank. Simple acts of acknowledgment, a handwritten note, flexible time off, or even a well-timed compliment does wonders.

Cultural Sensitivities: Consider how different cultures perceive and receive recognition. What is customary and respectful in one culture may not be in another.

Cultivating a Recognition-Rich Environment

To sum it all up, creating a culture in which recognition is ingrained and natural necessitates intentional actions and strategies. Here are a few steps to cultivate such an environment:

Leadership Training: Look for continuous training opportunities on the importance of recognition and how to effectively implement it.

Recognition Programs: Develop structured programs that encourage and facilitate regular recognition.

Feedback Mechanisms: Establish channels through which employees can provide feedback on the recognition they receive and suggest improvements.

Celebrate Milestones: Make it a habit to celebrate not just daily wins but also significant milestones, anniversaries, and personal achievements.

Crafting an Effective Recognition System

Alright, leaders, strap in! It's time to get our hands dirty with some real nuts-and-bolts leadership strategies to create and maintain a recognition system that not only acknowledges achievements but also fuels ongoing motivation and commitment. This isn't just about slapping together a few "Employee of the Month" awards and calling it a day. No, we're talking about a comprehensive, dynamic recognition system tailored to the unique needs and personalities of your team. Let's get into it!

The Blueprint for an Effective Recognition System

Creating a recognition system is like building a high-performance engine. It needs the right parts, regular maintenance, and fine-tuning to keep it running smoothly. Here's how you can build this engine from the ground up.

Step 1: Lay the Groundwork

Before you start handing out accolades, you need a solid foundation. This means understanding what motivates your team and what they value most.

> **Gather Input**: Start with the team. Surveys, one-on-ones, and informal chats can reveal what types of recognition they value most.
>
> **Define Objectives**: What do you want your recognition system to achieve? Are you looking to boost morale, increase productivity, enhance quality, or do all of the above? Clear objectives will guide your design and implementation.
>
> **Set Criteria**: Establish clear, achievable criteria for recognition. This ensures fairness and clarity in how rewards are given, and it helps employees understand what excellence looks like in your organization.

Step 2: Design the System

With your groundwork laid, it's time to start building the system. This stage is all about creating the mechanisms that will deliver recognition in a consistent, impactful way.

> **Choose the Types of Recognition**: From verbal acknowledgments and written thank-you notes to financial

bonuses and professional development opportunities, the types of recognition can vary. Choose a mix that aligns with your team's preferences and organization's culture.

Frequency and Timing: Decide how often and when recognition is given. While regular recognition keeps morale high, occasional surprise rewards can also have a powerful impact.

Make It Scalable: As your team grows, your recognition system should grow with it. Ensure that the system is scalable and adaptable to changing circumstances and new employees.

Step 3: Tailor Rewards to Individuals

A one-size-fits-all approach doesn't work when it comes to recognition. Tailoring rewards to fit individual employees' preferences shows that you understand and value them.

Personalized Rewards: Take time to personalize rewards based on the recipient's interests or needs. Consider offering a book to a team member who enjoys reading, or additional time off to an individual who prioritizes personal time.

Career-Related Rewards: For many employees, professional growth is a significant motivator. Consider offering rewards that contribute to their careers, such as a course or a conference they've been wanting to attend.

Peer Recognition: Enable and encourage peer-to-peer recognition. It's often just as valuable, if not more so, than recognition from leadership.

Step 4: Implement the System

Now that you've designed your system, it's time to put it into action. Implementation involves communicating the system to your team and starting the recognition process.

Communicate Clearly: Make sure everyone understands how the system works, what the criteria are, and how they can participate. Clear communication prevents misunderstandings and ensures broad buy-in.

Launch with a Bang: Kick off your new recognition system with an event or announcement that gets everyone excited. This initial boost can set a positive tone moving forward.

Train Your Leaders: Ensure leaders within your organization understand how to use the system effectively. They should know how to spot opportunities for recognition and how to deliver it in a way that aligns with the system's goals.

Step 5: Evaluate and Adjust

No system is perfect from the start. Regular evaluation and adjustment are key to maintaining its effectiveness over time.

Collect Feedback: Regularly solicit feedback from your team about the system's impact and any areas for improvement. You can conduct this through surveys, focus groups, or informal feedback channels.

Review and Refine: Use the feedback to make necessary adjustments. This might mean tweaking the types of rewards, the frequency of recognition, or even the criteria.

Celebrate Success: Don't forget to recognize and celebrate the success of the recognition system itself. Share how it has positively impacted the organization and the individuals in it.

Sustaining a Culture of Recognition

Implementing an effective recognition system is an ongoing journey, not a one-time setup. It's about continuously adapting to meet the evolving needs of your team and reinforcing a culture where recognition is woven into the fabric of daily work life. By following these steps and committing to regular evaluation and adjustment, you can ensure that recognition remains a powerful tool for enhancing motivation, satisfaction, and team cohesion.

Conclusion

There you have it—a deep dive into the transformative power of recognition. As we've explored, recognition isn't just about making people feel good; it's a strategic tool that can drive performance, enhance engagement, and build a resilient and committed workforce. So, take these insights, shake up your recognition game, and watch as your team's motivation, satisfaction, and value reach new heights. After all, in the world of effective leadership, recognizing someone's worth is not just nice to have; it's a must-have.

Chapter 6

Time Spent, Time Valued

"Good things happen not by managing time but by prioritizing attention."

- RICHIE NORTON
Award-Winning Author, Entrepreneur, and Speaker

We're diving into one of the most crucial yet often underestimated aspects of leadership—spending quality time with your team. In this fast-paced world, it's easy to get caught up in deadlines and to-do lists, but remember: time spent with your team is never wasted. It's an investment. And like any good investment, it takes quality time to yield substantial returns. Simultaneously, it's crucial for your employees to perceive their time as valued and to recognize the significance of regular and high-quality communication. This chapter will unpack the art of quality time, exploring its benefits for individual and team dynamics, and providing actionable strategies to make every moment count.

The Essence of Quality Time

When we talk about quality time in a leadership context, we're not just referring to the hours logged; we're talking about meaningful engagement that fosters trust, builds relationships, and enhances team cohesion. This kind of engagement is deliberate, focused, and, most importantly, empathetic. Your team should feel valued for their contributions and personalities.

Why Quality Time Matters

Quality time is the glue that holds teams together. It turns a group of individuals into a unified force. Here's why it's crucial:

Enhances Communication: Regular, meaningful interactions help break down barriers, leading to more open and honest communication.

Boosts Morale and Engagement: Employees who feel their leaders are genuinely invested in them are more motivated and committed to their work.

Fosters Mutual Trust: Spending time together allows both employees and leaders to build mutual trust, which is essential for a healthy work environment.

Facilitates Better Problem-Solving: Teams that spend quality time together understand each other's strengths and weaknesses, making them more effective at tackling challenges collaboratively.

Mastering One-on-One Interactions

One-on-one meetings are a cornerstone of quality time spent between a leader and their team members. These interactions are opportunities to connect on a deeper level, understand personal and professional goals, and address any concerns that might be on the table.

Regular Schedule: Set a regular cadence for one-on-ones. Whether it's weekly, bi-weekly, or monthly, consistency is key.

Create a Safe Space: Ensure that these meetings are a safe space where employees feel comfortable being open and honest without fear of judgment or reprisal.

Listen More Than You Speak: The primary goal of one-on-one time should be to listen. This is your chance to really hear what your employees are thinking and feeling.

Tailor the Experience: Customize based on the individual's needs. Some might need more guidance, while others might benefit from more freedom to express their ideas or concerns.

Powering Up with Team-Building Activities

Team-building activities are not just fun and games; they are a critical component in strengthening the group dynamic and enhancing cohesion. These activities should be engaging, inclusive, and aligned with your team's culture.

Diverse Activities: Mix it up with a range of activities that cater to different personalities and interests. From escape rooms to cooking classes, the key is to find activities that encourage collaboration and enjoyment.

Regular Intervals: Incorporate team-building exercises into your routine. It could be something small each month or a larger event each quarter.

Debrief and Feedback: After each activity, conduct a debrief session to discuss the lessons learned and collect feedback on the experience. This can help refine future activities and ensure they are providing value.

Creating Opportunities for Meaningful Engagement

Beyond meetings and structured activities, meaningful engagement can also occur through less formal interactions and spontaneous moments. Here's how you can create an environment that encourages such engagement:

Open-Door Policy: Reinforce an open-door policy where team members feel welcome to approach you with ideas, questions, or concerns at any time.

Shared Goals and Visions: Involve your team in setting goals and visions for their work and the organization. This inclusion makes every discussion more meaningful.

Celebrate Milestones: Celebrate personal and professional milestones. Whether it's a work anniversary, a personal achievement, or a project milestone, acknowledging these moments can greatly enhance relationship-building.

Encourage Cross-Departmental Interaction: Facilitate opportunities for your team to spend time with other departments. This not only broadens their network within the organization but also enhances their understanding of the business as a whole.

Time Spent, Time Valued

Leveraging Technology

In today's digital age, physical presence isn't always possible, especially in remote or hybrid work environments. Here's how you can still make quality time count:

Virtual Coffee Breaks: Schedule regular video calls where the sole purpose is to catch up on non-work-related matters.

Collaborative Tools: Utilize collaborative tools that allow for real-time interaction and cooperation on projects.

Regular Check-ins: Make use of chat applications for more frequent, informal check-ins.

Overcoming Challenges

While the benefits of spending quality time are numerous, there are challenges that leaders might face, such as finding the time in a packed schedule or engaging a diverse team with varied interests and personalities. Here's how to tackle:

Prioritize: Make quality time a non-negotiable part of your schedule. It's as important as any other strategic business activity.

Be Flexible: Recognize that one size does not fit all. Be flexible in how you interact with each team member and be willing to adjust your approach as needed.

Setting Priorities: The Cornerstone of Time Management

The first step in mastering time management is setting clear priorities. Knowing what needs your immediate attention and what can wait is crucial.

Identify High-Impact Activities: Determine which activities have the most significant impact on your team and organization. These should take precedence.

Urgent vs. Important: Use the Eisenhower Box technique to distinguish between tasks that are urgent versus important. Focus on what needs immediate attention and sticks.

Delegate Effectively: No leader can do everything alone. Delegation is not a sign of weakness, but rather a sign of a smart leader who knows how to allocate resources efficiently.

Scheduling Quality Interactions

Once you've set your priorities, the next step is making sure that spending quality time with your team is one of them. Here's how to schedule these crucial interactions without disrupting your workflow.

Regular Check-Ins: Block out regular times on your calendar for one-on-one meetings with your team members. This ensures that you remain consistently available to them and that they don't feel neglected.

Open Office Hours: Establish certain hours during the week when you're available for impromptu discussions. This flexibility encourages your team to come to you with fresh ideas or concerns that might not warrant a formal meeting.

Time Spent, Time Valued

Efficient Meetings: Keep your meetings efficient and on-point to avoid wasting time. Create a clear agenda for each meeting and stick to it to ensure that every minute spent in meetings is productive.

Time Management Strategies to Enhance Efficiency

Effective time management goes beyond handling tasks—it's about enhancing your overall leadership efficiency. Here are some strategies to help you manage your time better:

Time Blocking: Dedicate blocks of time to similar tasks in order to reduce context switching and increase focus. For example, set aside a block of time for reviewing reports, another for strategic planning, and another for team interactions.

Technology Tools: Leverage technology to save time. Use project management tools, scheduling software, and communication platforms to keep your tasks organized and communication clear.

Set Boundaries: Clearly define work hours for yourself and your team. This helps prevent work from spilling over into personal time, which is essential for your work-life balance.

Avoiding Burnout: Keeping Your Flame Alive

Leaders are especially prone to burnout due to the nature of their responsibilities. Here's how to manage your time effectively while keeping burnout at bay:

Recognize the Signs: Be aware of the early signs of burnout, such as chronic fatigue, irritability, or a decrease in job satisfaction. Recognizing these early can help you take steps to mitigate them before they worsen.

Take Breaks: Regular breaks throughout the day can improve your overall efficiency and mental health. Even a short walk or a few minutes of meditation can help reset your mind and reduce stress.

Seek Support: Don't hesitate to seek support from mentors, peers, or professionals if you feel overwhelmed. Leadership can be isolating, but you don't have to go it alone.

Conclusion

Quality time is one of the most significant investments you can make in your team. It strengthens bonds, builds trust, and fosters a supportive and collaborative workplace. By mastering one-on-one interactions, leading engaging team-building activities, and creating opportunities for meaningful engagement, you set your team—and your organization—up for success. Make every minute count and watch as your team transforms into a more cohesive, motivated, and productive unit.

Chapter 7

Personalized Presence
The Art of Being Fully Present

> *"Employees are a company's greatest asset - they're your competitive advantage. You want to attract and retain the best; provide them with encouragement, stimulus, and make them feel that they are an integral part of the company's mission."*
>
> **ANNE M. MULCAHY**
> Former CEO of Xerox

Welcome, leaders! In this chapter, we're going to explore a critical, yet often overlooked aspect of effective leadership—Personalized Presence. This isn't just about being physically in the same room as your team; it's about being mentally and emotionally engaged. It's about showing up for your employees in a way that resonates with each individual, understanding their unique needs, and adjusting your level of presence accordingly. Leadership presence is often described as a blend of poise, confidence, and authenticity that inspires confidence in others. It's about how you carry yourself, how you communicate, and how you make others feel. A leader with a strong presence can command a room without saying a word and make others feel heard and valued during interactions. Let's dive into why this is so crucial and how you can master the art of truly being there for your team.

The Power of Presence in Leadership

Presence is a powerful tool in the leadership toolkit. It's about more than just attendance; it's about engagement, attention, and connection. When leaders are fully present, they send a clear message: "You are important, and your contributions matter." This simple message can profoundly impact team dynamics, performance, and overall morale.

Why Personalized Presence Matters

Personalized presence goes one step further by recognizing that each team member has unique needs, communication styles, and expectations. Here's why it's essential:

Builds Trust: Being consistently present and attentive builds trust. Employees feel valued and understood, which strengthens their trust in leadership.

Enhances Communication: Effective communication relies on being present. This ensures you're not only hearing words but also understanding the emotions and intentions behind them.

Personalized Presence

Boosts Morale and Engagement: Employees are more engaged and motivated when they feel their leaders are genuinely interested in their well-being and professional growth.

Fosters a Supportive Environment: A leader who is attuned to the needs of their team can create a more supportive and inclusive workplace.

Understanding Levels of Presence

Each employee might require a different level of presence depending on their role, personality, and current projects. Here's how to adapt your presence to meet diverse needs:

The Newcomers: New employees might need more hands-on engagement as they navigate through the initial phases of their roles. Frequent check-ins and reassurances can help them feel supported.

The Independent Operators: Experienced employees, accustomed to working independently, may prefer less frequent but more in-depth interactions. Recognise their need for autonomy while remaining available when needed.

The Team Dependents: Some team members thrive on collaborative efforts and regular feedback. For these employees, ensure you're present in team settings and readily accessible.

The Remote Workers: Maintaining presence with remote employees requires deliberate efforts, such as regular video calls and virtual coffee chats, to bridge the physical distance.

Techniques for Active Listening

Active listening is at the heart of being present. It's not just about hearing words; it's about understanding the complete message being communicated. Here's how to hone your active listening skills:

Give Full Attention: Avoid distractions during conversations. This means no checking emails or glancing at your phone. Full attention shows that you value the speaker's words.

Reflect and Clarify: Paraphrase what's been said to ensure understanding. Ask clarifying questions if necessary. This shows that you are engaged and care about the details.

Non-Verbal Cues: Pay attention to body language, tone of voice, and facial expressions. These can provide insights into how the employee truly feels.

Empathy: Try to see things from the employee's perspective. Empathetic responses show that you are not just listening, but also feeling with them.

Recognizing Non-Verbal Cues

Non-verbal communication can tell you a lot about an employee's feelings and attitudes. Understanding these cues improves your ability to respond appropriately and modify your communication style.

Facial Expressions: Smiles, frowns, and furrowed brows can convey a lot about a person's emotions.

Posture and Gestures: Open gestures, leaning forward, or crossed arms all have meanings that can inform how comfortable or anxious a person is.

Eye Contact: Maintaining eye contact shows confidence and interest, while avoiding eye contact might suggest discomfort or distraction.

Impact on Employee Trust

Being fully present and attentive has a cumulative effect of deepening trust between you and your team. Trust is foundational in any relationship but is particularly crucial in a leadership context. Here's how presence influences trust:

Consistency: Being consistently present shows reliability, which is a cornerstone of trust.

Understanding: When leaders understand their employees' needs and respond appropriately, it reinforces the employee's trust in their leader's competence and empathy.

Safety: A leader who listens and responds to non-verbal cues creates a safer environment where employees feel they can express themselves without fear.

The Role of Mindfulness in Enhancing Presence

Mindfulness is a powerful tool for developing a leadership presence. It involves maintaining a moment-by-moment awareness of our thoughts, feelings, and surrounding environment. Here's how mindfulness can transform your leadership presence:

Improved Focus and Concentration: Regular mindfulness practice enhances your ability to concentrate and stay focused on the present moment. This is crucial in leadership, where distractions are plentiful and can lead to missed opportunities or overlooked details.

Enhanced Emotional Regulation: Mindfulness helps you recognize and regulate your emotions. This emotional awareness prevents your feelings from overpowering your actions or reactions, enabling you to handle stressful situations more calmly and effectively.

Better Decision Making: Being present and mindful allows you to make decisions based on clear, focused thought rather than impulsive reactions. This leads to more thoughtful and considered outcomes.

Increased Empathy and Understanding: Mindfulness enhances your ability to connect with others on a deeper level, improving empathy and thereby strengthening relationships within your team.

Reducing Distractions to Boost Presence

In our digital age, distractions are a constant. Here's how to minimize them to enhance your leadership presence:

Monitor Technology: Set specific times to check emails and messages rather than responding to notifications immediately. Using tech mindfully ensures it serves you, not controls you.

Organize Your Space: Keep your workspace clear of unnecessary clutter. A tidy, organized space can help reduce stress and improve focus.

Prioritize Tasks: Use the Eisenhower Box (urgent-important matrix) to prioritize tasks. This helps you stay focused on what truly matters and needs your attention.

Delegate: Empower your team by delegating tasks that do not require your direct involvement. This not only reduces your workload but also builds trust and develops your team's capabilities.

Fostering an Environment of Presence

Creating an environment that values presence can have a significant impact on your team's collective focus and productivity. Here are some strategies:

Lead by Example: Demonstrate presence in your actions. When you consistently show up fully, you set a standard for others to follow.

Encourage Breaks: Promote regular breaks among your team. Stepping away from work for short periods of time can help maintain concentration and reduce burnout.

Hold Mindfulness Sessions: Introduce mindfulness sessions for your team. This can be as simple as starting meetings with a one-minute meditation to center everyone's attention.

Create Quiet Zones: Establish areas in the workplace where employees can go to focus without distractions.

Conclusion: The Transformative Power of Presence

Personalized presence is not just a leadership strategy; it's a leadership commitment. It requires time, attention, and genuine interest in the people you lead. By mastering the art of presence—through active listening, recognizing non-verbal cues, and understanding the unique needs of your team—you can transform your leadership style and your workplace. It's about making every interaction count and ensuring your team knows they are heard, seen, and valued. With this approach, you don't just manage a team; you inspire and empower individuals to achieve their best, fostering a culture of trust, respect, and mutual success.

Chapter 8

Consideration

The Keystone of Compassionate Leadership

"Leadership is not a formula or a program, it is a human activity that comes from the heart and considers the hearts of others. It is an attitude, not a routine"

- DR. LANCE SECRETAN
Author, Actor, Speaker

In this chapter, we dive into one of the most crucial aspects of effective leadership—Consideration. This principle is not merely about listening or responding; it's about integrating empathy, respect, and genuine concern for the well-being and development of your team in every interaction. Consideration is the art of attuning yourself to the needs and feelings of others, valuing their perspectives, and making decisions that reflect a commitment to their personal and professional growth. This chapter explores the culture of consideration, offering strategies, and exercises to enhance your leadership effectiveness.

Consideration

The Essence of Consideration in Leadership

Consideration in leadership transcends basic people management skills; it involves understanding and addressing the emotional and professional needs of your team members. It's about creating an environment where employees feel genuinely cared for—not just as cogs in the machine, but as valuable individuals with unique contributions and aspirations.

Why Consideration Matters

Enhances Team Cohesion: When leaders exhibit consideration, it fosters a sense of community and belonging among team members, leading to enhanced cooperation and team spirit.

Boosts Morale and Motivation: Employees who feel their leaders truly care about them as individuals are more likely to feel motivated and committed to their work and the organization.

Improves Retention Rates: High levels of consideration reduce turnover rates, as employees are more likely to stay with a company that values and respects them.

Facilitates Open Communication: A considerate leadership approach encourages open lines of communication, making employees feel safe to share ideas, concerns, and feedback.

Cultivating a Culture of Consideration

Building a culture of consideration requires consistent effort and genuine commitment. Here's how to embed this principle deeply within your leadership practices:

Listening with Empathy

Active Listening: Move beyond hearing words to understanding the context and emotions behind them. This involves giving your full attention, asking clarifying questions, and reflecting back on what you've heard to ensure understanding.

Empathy: Try to put yourself in your employees' shoes, especially when they are facing challenges. Responding with empathy can significantly enhance the emotional well-being of your team.

Valuing Perspectives

Inclusivity in Decision Making: Involve team members in decisions that affect them. Solicit their input and genuinely consider their suggestions, which can lead to more innovative solutions and greater buy-in.

Diversity of Thought: Celebrate and encourage diverse viewpoints and ideas. Recognizing the value of different perspectives fosters an inclusive environment that is ripe for innovation.

Prioritizing Employee Well-being

Supportive Policies: Implement policies that reflect a commitment to employee well-being, such as flexible working hours, mental health days, and opportunities for professional development.

Regular Check-ins: Conduct regular one-on-one meetings not just to discuss work progress but to check in on their personal well-being and professional growth.

Case Studies: Consideration in Action

Case Study 1: Software Development Company
Situation: A leading software development company noticed a decline in team morale and productivity.

Actions Taken:
- **Listening Tours**: The CEO initiated 'listening tours' across the company, holding open forums and one-on-one sessions to gather employee concerns and suggestions.
- **Empathy Training**: All managers underwent training to improve their empathy and listening skills.
- **Well-being Programs**: Introduced well-being programs that included mental health resources and professional development workshops.

Outcome: There was a marked improvement in employee morale, a decrease in turnover rates, and a significant increase in productivity and innovation.

Case Study 2: Retail Corporation
Situation: A national retail chain faced issues with low employee satisfaction and high absenteeism.

Actions Taken:
- **Employee Feedback System**: Implemented a new feedback system that allowed employees to anonymously share their concerns and suggestions.

- **Flexible Scheduling**: Introduced flexible scheduling to accommodate the varying personal needs of employees.
- **Career Development Paths**: Developed clear career paths for employees, along with the necessary training and development opportunities to advance.

Outcome: Employee satisfaction scores improved, absenteeism decreased, and there was a noticeable enhancement in customer service quality.

Integration Strategies

To effectively integrate consideration into your leadership style, consider the following strategies:

Cultural Alignment: Ensure that your actions and policies are aligned with a culture of consideration. This might mean revisiting organizational values or mission statements to reflect this priority.

Leadership Development: Train leaders and managers within the organization on the importance of consideration and provide them with practical tools to implement it.

Feedback Mechanisms: Establish robust mechanisms for employees to provide feedback on their experiences and perceptions of consideration within the organization.

Action Plan to Demonstrate Consideration

Consideration in leadership goes beyond simple acts of kindness; it involves a deep, genuine commitment to understanding and prioritizing the well-being and development of employees. This commitment manifests in daily interactions and decision-making processes, significantly impacting team dynamics, trust, and loyalty. Here's how leaders can embed consideration into their day-to-day leadership practices to build stronger relationships and foster a trusting environment.

Active Listening

One of the most powerful ways a leader can demonstrate consideration is through active listening. This means giving full attention to the speaker, without planning your response while they are talking. It involves listening to understand, not just to reply.

Action Steps:
- During meetings, take notes to show you are engaged and to help you remember key points.
- Use reflective listening techniques, such as paraphrasing what the employee has said to confirm understanding. For example, say, "What I'm hearing is that you feel overwhelmed by the project deadlines. Is that correct?"
- Ask open-ended questions to encourage deeper conversation and show genuine interest in their thoughts and feelings.

Practicing Empathy

Empathy involves putting yourself in your employees' shoes and responding with sensitivity to their feelings. It's crucial for leaders to not only understand what employees are going through but also to convey that understanding back to them, affirming their feelings are valid and acknowledged.

Action Steps:
- Regularly check in with employees about how they are doing, both personally and professionally.
- Share your own experiences related to their struggles when appropriate, to demonstrate empathy and solidarity.
- When an employee expresses a concern, acknowledge the difficulty of the situation before jumping into problem-solving mode. Say something like, "It sounds like you're really stretched thin; let's figure out how we can adjust your workload."

Giving Constructive, Personalized Feedback:
Feedback is a crucial component of employee development and can significantly enhance or undermine their sense of being valued. Considerate leaders ensure that feedback is not only constructive but also personalized, focusing on the employee's specific growth and needs.

Action Steps:
- Schedule regular one-on-one feedback sessions, which can provide privacy and make the feedback feel more tailored and less formal.
- Start feedback sessions by highlighting what the employee does well before moving on to areas for improvement.
- Tailor feedback to the individual's career aspirations and personality. For example, for an employee who is very detail-oriented, you might focus on how their attention to detail saved a project from potential pitfalls.

Fostering Inclusive Decision-Making:
Being considerate also means involving team members in decisions that affect them. This not only improves the decisions through diverse input but also makes employees feel valued and respected.

Action Steps:
- When a new project or change initiative is proposed, gather input from the team to understand their perspectives and concerns.
- Create a transparent process for decision-making that allows all team members to contribute, such as using collaborative tools where everyone can submit ideas or vote on options.
- Explain the final decision and how you incorporated team input, which reinforces that their opinions were valued and considered.

Encouraging and Supporting Professional Development:
Consideration involves supporting the long-term career goals of employees. Leaders should actively facilitate opportunities for professional growth that align with the individual's aspirations.

Action Steps:
- Work with each employee to develop a growth plan that includes both short-term objectives and long-term goals.
- Provide resources for learning and development, such as access to courses, seminars, or workshops.
- Offer opportunities for new challenges and responsibilities that align with the employee's interests and growth plans.

Conclusion: Mastery Through Consideration

Consideration is not just a leadership skill—it's a leadership imperative. By mastering the art of empathetic listening, valuing diverse perspectives, and prioritizing the well-being and development of your team, you create an environment where employees feel respected, valued, and understood. This chapter has provided you with the strategies and tools to integrate consideration deeply and effectively into your leadership approach, ensuring that you not only meet the immediate needs of your team but also foster long-term loyalty, satisfaction, and engagement.

Chapter 9

Integrating the Leadership Language

"Be more concerned with your character than your reputation, because your character is what you really are, while your reputation is merely what others think you are."

- JOHN WOODEN
UCLA Basketball Coach, Presidential Medal of Freedom Recipient

Each principle plays a unique role in cultivating a positive organizational culture, enhancing team dynamics, and boosting overall performance. We'll explore practical strategies for blending these principles into a cohesive leadership approach, showcase insightful case studies, and guide you through reflective exercises to deepen your understanding and application. Think of these leadership principles as instruments in an orchestra. Each has its own distinct sound, but when played together, they create a harmonious symphony that captivates and inspires.

Here's how these principles interact with and complement each other:

Confirmation Affirmation and Recognition: These elements reinforce each other, with affirmation validating efforts and recognition celebrating them as they prefer, enhancing motivation and engagement.

Being of Service and Consideration: Service demonstrates your commitment to supporting team members' goals, while consideration ensures that this support is empathetically aligned with their well-being.

Time Spent, Time Valued and Personalized Presence: Dedicating quality time to each team member ensures that they feel valued, and tailoring this time to their specific needs deepens the connection and impact.

Case Studies: Integration in Action

These examples illustrate how effectively integrating these leadership languages can transform organizational culture and elevate team performance.

Case Study 1: Global Marketing Firm

Situation: A global marketing firm faced challenges with employee disengagement and high turnover.

Actions Taken:
- **Confirmation Affirmation**: Leaders began implementing regular feedback sessions, focusing on affirming employees' contributions to project successes.

- **Being of Service**: Managers actively worked alongside employees on major campaigns, providing hands-on support and guidance.
- **Consideration**: The firm introduced flexible working hours and remote working options to better accommodate personal employee needs.
- **Recognition**: Achievements were highlighted in monthly newsletters and annual award ceremonies.
- **Time Spent, Time Valued**: Managers scheduled weekly one-on-one meetings to discuss personal and professional development.
- **Personalized Presence**: Leaders practiced being fully present in all interactions, adapting their communication style to match each employee's preferences.

Outcome: The firm saw a notable decrease in turnover and a significant increase in employee satisfaction scores.

Case Study 2: Healthcare Provider

Situation: A healthcare provider struggled with low patient satisfaction scores and staff burnout.

Actions Taken:
- **Confirmation Affirmation**: Staff received personalized thank-you notes from management acknowledging their dedication, especially during peak times.
- **Being of Service**: Additional support staff were hired to assist during high-demand periods, alleviating some of the workload.
- **Consideration**: Management conducted regular wellness workshops aimed at addressing work-life balance.

- **Recognition**: Exceptional patient care was recognized in front of peers during staff meetings, with small tokens of appreciation given.
- **Time Spent, Time Valued**: Leaders spent time shadowing employees to better understand their daily challenges and needs.
- **Personalized Presence**: Executives maintained an open-door policy, encouraging staff to share concerns and suggestions freely.

Outcome: Patient satisfaction scores improved, and employee feedback reflected a better work environment and reduced feelings of burnout.

Integration Strategies

To effectively blend these principles into your leadership style, consider the following strategies:

Holistic Assessment: Regularly evaluate the needs and preferences of your team through surveys and direct conversations.

Adaptive Leadership: Always align your actions with the team's best interests by adjusting your leadership approach based on individual and situational needs.

Balanced Implementation: Craft a leadership plan that incorporates each of the six languages in balanced measures to address the diverse needs of your team.

Personal Reflection Exercises

Enhance your application of these principles through the following reflective practices:

Journaling: After significant interactions or decisions, reflect on how you applied the leadership languages and assess your approach's effectiveness.

Feedback Collection: Actively seek feedback from your team on your use of these principles and identify areas for improvement.

Role-Playing: Participate in role-playing exercises with your peers to practice different scenarios, with a focus on integrating multiple leadership languages.

Guide to Implementing Leadership Principles

This quick reference guide is designed to help you, the leader, implement the key principles we've discussed. This provides a detailed, step-by-step action plan, complete with actionable steps, self-assessment tools, and goal-setting templates. Following this structured approach will equip you to enhance your leadership skills systematically and sustainably. Each principle requires thoughtful integration into your leadership practice. Here's how to do it effectively:

Step 1: Self-Assessment and Awareness

Before implementing any new strategies, it's crucial to understand your current standing. Self-assessment helps in identifying areas of strength and those needing improvement.

Integrating the Leadership Language

Action Steps:
1. **Conduct a Self-Assessment**: Use tools like the Leadership Practices Inventory (LPI) to evaluate your current use of the leadership language principles.
2. **Seek Feedback**: Gather feedback from peers, supervisors, and direct reports to gain a comprehensive view of your leadership effectiveness.
3. **Reflect on Feedback**: Analyze the feedback and assessment results to pinpoint specific areas for improvement.

Tools:
- Self-Assessment Checklists for each principle.
- 360-Degree Feedback forms.

Step 2: Goal Setting

Clear, actionable goals are essential for effective leadership development. Setting SMART (Specific, Measurable, Achievable, Relevant, Time-bound) goals ensures that you can track your progress and achieve meaningful improvements.

Action Steps:
1. **Define Specific Goals**: Based on the self-assessment, define specific goals for each leadership principle. For example, increase team recognition practices by 50% within the next quarter.
2. **Break Down Goals**: Decompose each goal into manageable tasks and activities.
3. **Assign Timelines**: Set realistic deadlines for each task to maintain momentum and focus.

Tools:
- SMART Goal Templates.
- Goal Breakdown Worksheets.

Step 3: Developing Action Plans

With clear goals in place, the next step is to develop detailed action plans for each principle. This involves outlining specific strategies and actions to meet your goals.

Action Steps:
1. **Plan for Each Principle**: Create a unique action plan for Confirmation Affirmation, Being of Service, Consideration, Recognition, and Time Spent, Time Valued.
2. **Identify Resources Needed**: Determine what resources (time, budget, personnel) are needed to implement.
3. **Schedule Regular Reviews**: Set up regular intervals (e.g., monthly or quarterly) to review progress against goals and adjust plans as necessary.

Tools:
- Action Plan Templates.
- Resource Allocation Templates.

Step 4: Implementation

The implementation phase is where plans turn into action. Effective implementation requires commitment, flexibility, and ongoing support.

Action Steps:
1. **Engage Your Team**: Communicate your goals and plans with your team. Their buy-in is crucial for success.

2. **Start Small**: Begin with pilot tests of your strategies in smaller groups before a full-scale roll-out.
3. **Monitor Progress**: Keep a close watch on the progress of your action plans and make adjustments as needed.

Tools:
- Implementation Checklists.
- Progress Tracking Dashboards.

Step 5: Evaluation and Adjustment

Ongoing evaluation is key to understanding the impact of your leadership changes and making necessary adjustments.

Action Steps:
1. **Evaluate Outcomes**: Regularly evaluate the outcomes of your leadership actions against the set goals.
2. **Solicit Feedback**: Continuously gather feedback from your team on the changes and their impact.
3. **Adjust Strategies**: Based on evaluation and feedback, make necessary adjustments to your strategies to better meet your goals.

Tools:
- Evaluation Forms.
- Feedback Collection Tools.

Step 6: Fostering Continuous Improvement

Leadership development is an ongoing journey. Continuous improvement ensures that your leadership practices remain effective and responsive to changing circumstances.

Action Steps:
1. **Commit to Learning**: Dedicate time to ongoing learning and development in leadership skills.
2. **Stay Updated**: Keep informed about the latest research and developments in leadership theories and practices.
3. **Repeat the Cycle**: Regularly revisit the steps in this action plan to refine and enhance your leadership approach.

Tools:
- Professional Development Plans.
- Leadership Learning Resources.

Your Roadmap to Effective Leadership

This action plan provides an approach to integrating and mastering the leadership language. By following these steps and committing to continuous improvement, you can improve not only your leadership effectiveness but also your team's overall productivity and morale. Remember, effective leadership is not a destination but a journey of constant learning and adaptation. Let this action plan be your guide as you navigate the path to becoming a more effective, considerate, and respected leader.

Integrating these leadership languages into a unified approach is key to developing a leadership style that is not only effective but also deeply respected. This holistic approach not only leads to increased productivity and satisfaction but also fosters a culture of loyalty and innovation, propelling your team towards sustained success.

Chapter 10

Sustaining and Adapting Long-Term Strategies

"Good business leaders create a vision, articulate the vision, passionately own the vision, and relentlessly drive it to completion"

- JACK WELCH
Former CEO of General Electric

Organizations face constant changes in market conditions, employee expectations, and technological advancements. Thus, your leadership must also evolve. This chapter is dedicated to helping maintain the effectiveness of the leadership languages while staying responsive to emerging trends and shifting needs within your team.

The Importance of Long-Term Sustainment

Effective leadership is not static; it's a dynamic skill that must adapt over time to remain relevant and impactful. Sustaining your leadership effectiveness involves not only maintaining the foundational practices you have established but also continuously refining and expanding them to meet new challenges.

Continuous Improvement in Leadership

Continuous improvement is the heartbeat of long-lasting leadership success. It involves a commitment to consistently assessing and enhancing your leadership practices based on feedback, outcomes, and changing environments. In the realm of effective leadership, continuous improvement is not merely a strategy—it's a necessity, especially when it comes to building and maintaining relationships with employees. This section delves into why continuous improvement is crucial for fostering strong, lasting relationships underpinned by the leadership languages.

Why Continuous Improvement Matters

Leadership, at its core, is about relationships. The quality of these relationships can significantly impact everything, from team morale and employee retention to productivity and overall organizational success. Here's why it's vital:

Evolving Employee Expectations: As the workplace continues to evolve, so do the expectations of employees. What worked yesterday might not be enough today. Leaders need to continually adapt their approaches to meet these changing needs, ensuring that their leadership remains relevant and effective.

Deepening Trust: Trust is built when leaders consistently show that they are committed to growth—both their own and their team members. By engaging in continuous improvement, leaders demonstrate their commitment to personal and professional development, reinforcing trust.

Enhancing Communication: Continuous improvement often involves refining communication skills. Effective communication is critical to understanding and addressing employee needs, providing appropriate feedback, and articulating company visions clearly.

Continuous Improvement in Relationship Building

To effectively implement continuous improvement, leaders can adopt the following strategies:

Regular Feedback Mechanisms

Implementing regular and structured feedback mechanisms allows leaders to gather insights into employee satisfaction, uncover areas for improvement, and adjust their strategies to better align with their team's needs.

Action Steps:

1. **Establish Regular Feedback Sessions**: Schedule monthly or quarterly feedback sessions with team members to discuss their concerns, ideas, and feelings about the workplace.
2. **Anonymous Surveys**: Use surveys to collect feedback about leadership effectiveness and team dynamics.

Personal Development Plans

Personal development plans not only focus on the professional growth of employees but also show that leaders care about their personal aspirations. This can strengthen relationships and improve employee engagement.

Action Steps:
1. **Individualized Growth Opportunities**: Work with each team member to create personalized development plans that align with their career goals and interests.
2. **Mentorship Programs**: Develop mentorship programs that pair less experienced employees with more seasoned colleagues, fostering a culture of learning and support.

Adapting Leadership Styles
Different situations and team members may require different approaches. Leaders who adapt their styles to meet the specific needs and preferences of their team members can improve understanding and cooperation.

Action Steps:
1. **Leadership Flexibility Training**: Invest in training to learn how to effectively switch between leadership styles.
2. **Situational Leadership Assessments**: Regularly assess which situations benefit from certain styles and adapt as needed.

Continuous Learning and Innovation
Staying informed about the latest leadership theories and practices can help leaders find new and effective ways to connect with and support their team members.

Action Steps:
1. **Ongoing Education**: Enroll in leadership workshops, seminars, and courses.
2. **Innovation Implementation**: Stay open to implementing innovative leadership tools and techniques that might enhance team dynamics.

Sustaining and Adapting Long-Term Strategies

Adapting to Changing Employee Needs

As generations shift and technological advancements change the workplace landscape, the needs and expectations of employees also evolve. Adapting your leadership to these changes is crucial for maintaining team engagement and productivity.

Action Steps:
1. **Stay Informed on Workforce Trends**: Keep abreast of the latest research and trends in workplace dynamics, employee satisfaction, and organizational health.
2. **Regular Team Assessments**: Conduct annual or bi-annual team assessments to understand the changing needs and expectations of your employees.
3. **Flexible Leadership Styles**: Be prepared to adjust your leadership style and strategies to better align with the needs of your team. This may involve shifting more heavily into one leadership language while pulling back on another, depending on the current team dynamics and organizational goals.

Staying Current with Leadership Trends

The field of leadership is continuously evolving, influenced by global trends, technological advancements, and cultural shifts. Staying current with these trends is essential for keeping your leadership practices relevant and effective.

Action Steps:

1. **Industry Involvement**: Participate in industry groups, forums, and associations to stay connected with current leadership discussions and innovations.
2. **Ongoing Education**: Engage in continuous learning through advanced degrees, certifications, or informal learning paths like online courses or webinars.
3. **Innovative Experimentation**: Be open to experimenting with new leadership tools, techniques, and technologies as they emerge. Pilot these innovations in controlled settings to gauge their effectiveness before a broader rollout.

Long-Term Planning and Goal Setting

Sustaining and adapting leadership requires foresight and planning. Developing long-term goals and strategies ensures that leadership remains proactive rather than reactive.

Action Steps:

1. **Develop a Five-Year Leadership Plan**: Outline where you want your leadership to be in the next five years, including what principles you aim to enhance and what new competencies you need to develop.
2. **Strategic Review Sessions**: Hold annual strategic review sessions to evaluate your progress towards these long-term goals and make necessary adjustments.
3. **Succession Planning**: Part of long-term leadership sustainability involves planning for succession. Develop and mentor future leaders within your organization to ensure that the leadership languages continue to thrive beyond your tenure.

Conclusion: Your Legacy of Evolving Leadership

The journey of leadership does not have a final destination; it is a continuous path of growth, adaptation, and reinvention. By committing to the long-term strategies outlined in this chapter, you ensure that your leadership remains effective and responsive to the needs of your organization and team. The leadership languages—Confirmation Affirmation, Being of Service, Consideration, Recognition, Time Spent, Time Valued, and Personalized Presence—are not just tools for today; they are investments in your future and the future of those you lead. Embrace these strategies, adapt to the evolving landscape, and build a legacy of leadership that stands the test of time.

Chapter 11

Wrap-Up & Final Thoughts

"Of all the things that sustain a leader over time, love is the most lasting. The best-kept secret of successful leaders is love: staying in love with leading, with the people who do the work, with what their organizations produce, and with those who honor the organization by using its work."

- JAMES KOUZES AND BARRY POSNER
Co-Authors of The Leadership Challenge

As we draw close to the end of our journey through the exploration of the leadership language, let's pause to reflect on what we have learned and the steps we can take moving forward. Leadership is much more than a mere position or title; it is an ongoing commitment to growth, understanding, and genuine engagement with those we lead. Throughout this book, we have delved deeply into the critical leadership languages. Each of these languages plays a vital role in creating a harmonious and effective workplace where every team member feels valued and understood.

Confirmation Affirmation
Preferred way of recognizing and validating an employee's contributions, opportunities, and potential, strengthening their confidence and commitment

Being of Service
The degree of support and assistance an employee desires, demonstrated in the leader's ability to actively help achieve goals and objectives.

Recognition
Desired level of acknowledgment of employees' achievements and efforts, which fosters motivation, satisfaction, and a sense of value within the team.

Time Spent, Time Valued
Dedicating the appropriate amount of quality time to each employee to address their needs while validating the time spent provided value for their priorities.

Personalized Presence
Level of attentiveness and engagement with each employee, understanding their unique needs and preferences, and fostering a deeper, more meaningful connection.

Consideration
Attentively listening to employees' concerns, valuing their perspectives, and making thoughtful decisions that prioritize their well-being and development.

Inspiring Action and Continuous Growth

As leaders, our journey is never complete; there is always room for growth and improvement. The concepts discussed are not end goals but starting points for developing a richer, more nuanced approach to leadership. Here are some thoughts to inspire you to take action:

Embrace the Journey of Leadership
Leadership is a journey, not a destination. Each day offers a new opportunity to learn something new about yourself, your team, and the world around you.

Lead with Empathy and Integrity
At the heart of leadership is the ability to connect with others genuinely and empathetically. Strive to understand the unique needs and aspirations of those you lead and address them with integrity and sincerity. The most respected leaders are those who treat their team with fairness and respect.

Foster a Culture of Openness and Innovation
Establish a welcoming environment for new ideas and a safe space for team members to voice their thoughts and concerns. A culture of openness and innovation not only drives the organization forward but also fosters a sense of community and shared purpose.

Commit to Lifelong Learning
The best leaders are perpetual learners. Commit yourself to continuous learning—be it through books, workshops, courses, or everyday experiences. Every interaction and every challenge is an opportunity to learn and grow.

Leave a Lasting Impact
As a leader, consider what legacy you want to leave behind. How will you impact the lives of those you lead? Strive to leave behind a legacy of kindness, strength, and inspiration—a legacy that encourages others to aspire to greater heights.

Embracing Love as the Core of Leadership

As we bring our exploration of the leadership languages to a close, let's circle back to a foundational concept that underpins all these principles—love. While often not spoken about explicitly in corporate environments, love in leadership is about demonstrating genuine care, commitment, and compassion towards the people you lead. It's about fostering an environment where each team member feels valued, understood, and supported.

By integrating love with the leadership languages we see a framework for what it truly means to lead with love. Remember, this is not a task to check off, but a lifestyle that embodies how you will demonstrate your ability to lead. It impacts your attitude and behaviors, influencing your actions, leaving a legacy of leadership success that others want to emulate. Many times, it takes just one person to be the spark of inspiration and courage to put yourself out there and show that love will always prevail no matter the circumstances. Here's how you can use the leadership languages to build your courageous leadership identity:

Love in Confirmation Affirmation: When you affirm someone's efforts and potential, you are expressing your belief in their capabilities and value. This form of encouragement is a manifestation of love that empowers individuals, boosting their confidence and commitment.

Love in Being of Service: Acts of service go beyond mere assistance; they are acts of selflessness where the leader puts the needs of others first. This kind of support is a powerful expression of love that builds deep trust and loyalty.

Love in Consideration: Attentively listening to and valuing employees' perspectives is a respectful acknowledgment of their worth. This thoughtful attention to their well-being and development is a clear demonstration of love that fosters a positive and supportive work environment.

Love in Recognition: Acknowledging and celebrating achievements is an act of love that affirms their contributions are invaluable. Recognition makes team members feel appreciated and valued, enhancing satisfaction and motivation.

Love in Time Spent, Time Valued: Dedicating time to genuinely engage with each team member shows that you care about them as individuals, not just as employees. This investment of time is a fundamental act of love that validates their importance to the organization and to you, personally.

Love in Personalized Presence: Being fully present and attentive during interactions shows a deep level of respect and care. It signifies that you are genuinely interested in their thoughts and feelings, a direct expression of love that strengthens connections.

Wrap-Up & Final Thoughts

Integrating love into the fabric of your leadership through the languages we have explored doesn't just enhance your effectiveness—it transforms the lives of those you lead. It fosters an environment where people feel safe, respected, and motivated to give their best. As you reflect on the principles discussed and the strategies outlined, consider how each action and decision can be infused with love.

The legacy you leave as a leader is not measured by the targets met or the profits earned, but by the impact you have on the hearts and minds of those you lead. Lead with love, and watch as it reverberates through your team, your organization, and beyond, creating a culture where everyone thrives together. This is the true essence of transformative leadership.

Final Thoughts: The Power of Inspired Leadership
Leadership can be a powerful force for change, inspiring others to achieve their best and fostering an environment where everyone can thrive. Let your leadership be a light that guides and a force that empowers. Stand firm in your values, lead with your heart and your head, and never underestimate the power of inspired leadership to change the world.

Thank you for embarking on this journey of exploration and discovery in the art of leadership. May the lessons you've learned inspire you to new heights of success and fulfillment, both as a leader and as a champion for your team.

www.ingramcontent.com/pod-product-compliance
Lightning Source LLC
Chambersburg PA
CBHW030443220526
45464CB00006B/2401